Stop the World, I Want to Get Off.

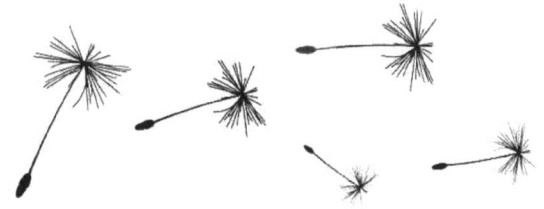

By

Jacky Power

Copyright © Jacky Power 2022
This book is sold subject to the condition that it shall not, by way of trade or otherwise, be lent, resold, hired out, or otherwise circulated without the publisher's prior consent in any form of binding or cover other than that in which it is published and without a similar condition including this condition being imposed on the subsequent publisher.
The moral right of Jacky Power has been asserted.
ISBN-13: ISBN 978-1-7397132-0-1

For you, of course.

Words for when you want to leave the planet but don't have billions to build a rocket.

CONTENTS

AUTHOR'S NOTE 1
   ONCE UPON A TIME 2

REASON 1: THE WORLD HAS GONE TO SHIT **4**
   THE WORLD HAS GONE TO SHIT 5
   IN THIS TIME OF FRUSTRATION 6
   LOCKDOWN LOONIES 7
   THE GIFTS OF LOCKDOWN 9
   CHRISTMAS WITHOUT YOU IS: A RESPONSE 10
   WORLD LEADER DESPAIR 11
   THE PRE-NUP 12
   IN MEMORY OF THE FRONT-LINE WORKERS 13
   LOCKDOWN REVIEW 14

REASON 2: THE PROCESS OF GETTING OLDER **15**
   THE DAY OF BIRTH DISEASE 16
   I DID A VART IN YOGA 18
   A PUBLIC SERVICE ANNOUNCEMENT 19
   MUMMY DANCING 20
   BIRTHDAY UN-LAMENT 21

REASON 3: SO MUCH STUFF IN THE WORLD **22**
   BE A LITTER PICKER UPPER 23
   GREENWASHING 24
   THE SÉANCE 25
   ALL AT SEA 26

REASON 4: HOW WE LOOK AT MENTAL HEALTH **27**
   THE EXPERT 28
   LABELS 29
   POPPY 30
   MAX 31

REASON 5: NOT GIVING SPACE FOR PEOPLE TO FEEL THEIR FEELINGS 32

    WHEN I SAY I'M FEELING LOW LOW 33
    DROWNING TO LIVE 34
    IF YOU NEED IT TODAY 35

REASON 6: THE WORLD OF PUBLISHING 36

    BITTERNESS 37
    TO MY MUSE 38
    A VIEW ON POETRY FROM 39
    MY TEENAGE SELF 39
    DRAGON SLAYER 40
    KEEP GOING 41

REASON 7: APPARENTLY SOME OF US DON'T MATTER 42

    ODD SOCKS 44
    TONE DEAF 45
    LOVE AND LIGHT 46
    MAGAZINE MANTRAS 47
    TRUE SELF-LOVE 48
    SUNDAY LOVE SONGS 50
    INSTA-SELFIE-SATION 51
    FREE THINKING 52
    THE DYSLEXIC KID 53
    THE WEED 54
    LESSONS FROM NATURE 55

REASON 8: PEOPLE 56

    THE COMMUTE 57
    I AM LONELY 59
    BELONGING 60

REASON 9: ILLNESS 61

    TO MR LUKE KEEMIA 62
    WHAT MISERY IS THIS? 63

STOP TELLING ME 65
IT'S NOT FAIR 66
AND THEN 68

REASON 10: FEAR AND DESPAIR 69

TO MY FEAR 71
THERE IS BEAUTY IN DESPAIR 72
RESOLVE 73
OUR MOONLIT PATH 74
DON'T JUMP IN THE PUDDLES! 75
THE SURREY COMMUNITY FRIDGE 76
MIDDLE-AGED BOOTCAMP 77
TRAUMA THRIVERS 78
THE GIFT OF POETRY 80
THE HUNT FOR HOPE 81

ACKNOWLEDGEMENTS 82

ABOUT THE AUTHOR 84

AUTHOR'S NOTE

Hello! This book is based on a show that I did in October 2021 called *Stop the World, I Want to Get Off*, as part of a local arts festival called Mole Valley Arts Alive in Surrey, UK.

I thought I'd pop it into a book (as you do), because some of the poems are related to Covid and I think that if I don't get them out now then their relevance may shrivel up like a long-forgotten grape in a lunch box.

I did another show, as part of Mole Valley Arts Alive in 2019, which was about how tricky it is to be human. Things were a doddle back then though, weren't they? The year 2020, well, that was a real slap in the face! I wrote the poem *Once Upon a Time*, one morning when it all felt pretty bleak.

Looking through the poems that I had written during this time of Covid, uncertainty and disappointment, I knew I couldn't be alone in feeling the way I did. I often write when I feel unsure, scared or alone and sometimes balance it up with a bit of humour in the writing, even when I'm dealing with tricky subjects. Or maybe it is *because* I am dealing with tricky subjects that I need to lighten things up a bit.

After months of separation, due to lockdown, I had the chance of doing another show. There are so many discombobulations right now that I decided to call the show *Stop the World, I Want to Get Off*.

When I'm feeling fearful, I have a choice. I can either believe it, feed it, watch it grow ears and fangs and viciousness, or I can look it right in the eye and sing it a song. That is what my poems do.

In this book I share these top ten reasons why I want to stop the world and get off. I wonder if you can relate!

Once Upon A Time

'Once Upon A Time' was a washed-up hag,
Her face all raw, her boobs all sagged.
'Happy Ever After', her faithful beau,
Exposed as a fraud (it had all been for show).
The audience gasped: afraid, distraught.
What's left now? was their collective thought.
'I' stood up in the eye of the storm,
Around her collecting a funny new norm.
She picked up her pen and wrote a note,
It's time to repeat it here by rote...

No magic, no spells, no witches, no potions.
It's time to get rid of these fanciful notions!
No heroes, no knights, no valiant fights.
It's time to get rid of these dizzying sights.
We're in a dismantling,
Destructing the old;
A complete departure from
The tales we were told.

We won't find our answers
In fighting the Other.
The secret key to loving each other
Is the lonely journey into the self.
You won't find *this* story on the fairy tale shelf.

Stalk your dragons within and slay them down dead!
That is what's needed for the times ahead.
There is no beginning, the ending's not sure,
Just hold on to the present to stay secure.
Whisper this truth to those who can hear.
Take hold of your faith, take hold of your fear,
And know that each stumble, each footstep you take
Is how we rebuild and how we remake.

REASON 1:

THE WORLD HAS GONE TO SHIT

The first reason really sums up what 2020 was like. It was the first year which was totally overshadowed by Covid. The pandemic affected all of us in some way. It completely disrupted our lives, with lockdowns, homeschooling, daily updates and new terminology.

In 2020 news bulletins were relentless with the fallout of climate change, political turbulence and social injustice. Christmas was all but cancelled and we all hoped that, by the simple change of the year date, 2021 would be different. That year, though, started with news of the Capitol Hill riots.

To sum it up, it can feel like the world has gone to shit.

The World Has Gone to Shit

The world has gone to shit, it has,
The world has gone to shit!
A discombobulation, is sweeping through our nation
As shoppers binge on bog roll and tinned food.
Apocalyptic thoughts, as we stockpile what we've bought,
As we spiral into stratospheric panic!
But...
Let's stop for a sec,
To breathe in,
To reflect.
It's not possible to sustain a life so manic.
Resistance to what's true, causes suffering (that's not new).
What if you allow yourself some slack?
For just five minutes, smell the flowers;
A glimpse of calm amongst the hours
Of stress and doubt and worldwide updates coming in.
Put down your phone and walk away:
Press a pause on your dismay,
And remember that, in this moment,
We're still living.

In This Time of Frustration

In this time of frustration
At the Covid complication,
'Unprecedented' in our nation
That's brought such isolation
And worldwide cessation.
It's surely an indication:
A Godly declaration,
A cosmic education,
That we need a transformation:
An enhanced imagination,
A call for activation.
Indeed, an obligation!
A time for rehabilitation.
A relegation of justification,
To humanely address migration,
Own up to discrimination,
Stop Earth's brutalisation,
Heal our separation.
This time of innovation
To create a civilisation
That could be a real salvation.

Lockdown Loonies

Shush!
No!
I won't tell you who I'm texting.
Oh my God! It's so perplexing,
The lack of space that I've been getting
In lockdown.

The stream of inane questions,
Hasn't faltered, hasn't lessened
As my kids have just been
Constantly around.

Of course, I truly love them.
I'm just impatient to know when
I'll get some sort of a life back
Of my own!

To be able to pee in peace...
Can I get a day release?
For the good behaviour I've managed
Up till now?

My shouts have been into pillows.
I haven't screamed, I haven't bellowed,
But time, well, I think
It's running out.

And just as the school term's ending
Where home schooling's been mind-bending,
Now the summer holidays
Are here!

There's no ending to this rhyme…
Just a movement over time…
From what was then, to well, I guess to
What is now.

So, if you identify with this,
Give a wave! Blow a kiss!
We'll all get through this
Craziness…

… somehow.

The Gifts of Lockdown

The presents are wrapped under the tree.
What delights are in store? Well now, let's see!
Mary's gifted her self-published book!
Two hundred pages on how to cook...
Banana bread.
Bob's bottle of homemade wine,
The grape crushing used up lockdown time.
Delicious.
Clare's knitted a scarf and a half,
It's the perfect fit for a tall giraffe.
Just what was needed.
Catherine's homemade potpourri;
A scent of jojoba and matcha tea.
Exquisite.
Sam thinks he's too hot to handle...
Probably why he made a 'revive' soy candle.
Intriguing.
Jessie's fashioned paperclips
Into a belt that skims hips.
So creative.
John's gone for a homemade mask,
From spare loo roll, it was quite a task.
Inspiring.
Jen's perfume smells like sanitiser.
Shush, don't tell her, she'll be none the wiser.
So naughty.
Shop-bought trinkets are long forgotten,
With the gifts of lockdown – we've been spoilt rotten!

Christmas Without You Is: A Response

A turkey with no stuffing.
A puff pastry mince pie in need of puffing.
A mulled wine missing all the cloves.
A Rudolph reindeer with no red nose.
An elf on the shelf who's not moved for days.
A present this year that was last year's craze.
A nativity scene without the stable.
A vacant chair at the laden table.
A present you've wrapped with no sticky-backed plastic.
Christmas loungewear with no elastic.
An avocado with no prawn.
A Jennifer without a Dawn.
An Aled without a Snowman.
A cold steamed pudding without a saucepan.
A merrily on low.
A snowball, without the snow.
A buck's fizz with no... fizz.
That's what Christmas without you is.

I wrote this poem in response to Brian Bilston's poem 'Christmas without you is'.

World Leader Despair

Each time you
Argue your case
From another
Faltering point of view,
I don't see your mental agility;
Just your moral fragility
And your inability for any
Gentility,
Stability,
Tranquillity…
Your hostility
Is the final
Nail in the coffin
Of your
Public utility.

The Pre-nup

Dear 2021,
Look, I know we've not begun,
But there's a few things
I need to get straight
Before we get into our first date.
You see, my hindsight's 2020.
My ex, well, he left me feeling empty
Of peace and hope and friends and squeezes:
Floods and fires, riots, diseases
Were more his penchant for affection.
It was a shit storm, upon reflection.
So now I'm looking for a new direction.
Look, I'm realistic! I don't need perfection,
Just a chance of reconnection.
So in the spirit of my protection
I'd like to bring to your attention
This prenup – just need a squiggle here...
No! Sign it RIGHT now! There's a dear...

(Unfortunately, I think this got lost in the post!)

In Memory of the Front-Line Workers

It's easy in the rush,
In the frenzy, in the rumble,
Easy to forget my debt,
To be grateful, to be humble.
To spend a moment, such little time,
To give thanks that I call freedom mine.
Lest we forget, the lads, the lasses,
Who gave their lives to heal the masses.

On review though, I was lucky. We managed to escape Covid in the first year, my husband's work continued and I was in a position where I could stop working, to focus on the home-schooling of our kids. The turbulence outside our home seemed to come from every angle, but at home, we managed to ride the Corona-coaster.

Lockdown Review

I didn't learn a new instrument,
But I did fashion a face mask from an old pair of jeans
(just one).

I didn't write a book,
But I did wash gazillions of underpants
(and matched rogue pairs of socks).

I didn't pause and pivot, birthing a thriving business,
But I did care for the children I had birthed
(and sometimes they even laughed a lot).

I didn't make kombucha or ferment anything,
But I did drink copious cups of coffee
(and sometimes I also made a cup for my husband).

I didn't do anything to become a national hero
But I did make it this far
(Thank God).

REASON 2:

THE PROCESS OF GETTING OLDER

Ageing, of course, starts with having your birthday, and that's it, you see, we are already falling at the first hurdle, because some people in our family suffer from The Day of Birth Disease. Birthdays can be tricky as we get older. I find that I flip between wanting to celebrate and wanting to hide.

It's not just birthdays, but the ageing process on my body in general. It can feel like a lot of loss. A loss of dignity, being able to do things easily and... dance moves.

The Day of Birth Disease

'I'm afraid,' the doc looks me in the eye,
'It's such grave news indeed.
You see your son is suffering from
The day of birth disease.'

'The day of birth disease!' I cry.
'What ever can you do?
Is there a cure? I need to know!
And please, explain it too.'

'You see,' the doc confides in me,
'Your son is seeking worth
From the fuss that you make of him
When you celebrate his birth.

He feels that, for this day at least,
He should be treated like a prince.'
I'm startled at this shocking news
before I slowly start to wince.

'I recognise these symptoms, doc!
I've suffered all my life!
I didn't know it was hereditary,
Let me share with you my strife.

I felt that way when growing up,
Worked hard not to pass it on.
How can it be that, despite all this
The damage has been done?

I blew balloons and sang out loud
Each birthday that went by.
I built him up year on year.'
I deflate and breathe a sigh.

'You tried too hard but once a year,'
The doc advises me.
'It's not about grand gestures.
It's your love he needs to see.

Make sure his voice is equally heard
Amongst your chaotic crew...'
'It's tough juggling three kids,' I say,
'So tell me what to do.'

'Take interest in his dreams and plans,
Say, "I believe in you,"
And when you see him doubt himself
Help him find his own way through.

Don't label him as this or that,
Delight in the soul you see.
You may be able to manage it
And set this poor child free.

Even when we try so hard
Not to pass our baggage on
It pops up anyway somewhere,
That's life, now carry on.'

I Did A Vart In Yoga

I did a vart in yoga.
I've had 3 kids you see,
It started as a tiny squeak
As I went to lift my knee.
I thought I'd got away with it,
But later we did plow
And that was when I let rip -
Like the bellow of a cow.

I sat up like a meerkat
To come out of this dangerous pose,
And then I spotted the teacher
with her hand upon her nose.
I tried to make some gestures,
to explain my plight;
All whilst attempting warrior 3,
That really was a sight.

Shavasana came not soon enough,
after which I ran out quick.
It's not something I'll be showing off
as my new found party trick.
I won't be going back there,
but I'm not taking it to heart,
I'll train as a yoga teacher,
only teaching those who vart.

A Public Service Announcement

Do you pee-pee during PT? Is your pelvic floor in the basement?
Do you cross your legs each time you sneeze? Have your lady bits had a displacement?

Are you lamenting your star jumps are numbered? Your burpees not perky no more?
Those latch key moments too close a shave, as you try to rush through the front door?

Do you think you're resigned to... Pilates? Boot camp a thing of the past?
Is it only the broadband in your house that could now be counted as fast?

Embrace this new phase with gusto! Adaption is what we must do!
Who can help us without any fuss though? Why, your gynae physio, that's who!

They won't take the piss (that's a bad pun). They'll keep you strong, trim and still fit.
You don't have to suffer in silence. So do what you must, but don't quit!

Mummy Dancing

I'm not accusing you of theft,
It's just, my dance moves… well, they've left.
My left foot doesn't know what's right,
And now my feet don't dance – they fight.
My mojo that would make me move
Has been derailed from its groove.
I used to bump and grind and twerk,
But now I shuffle, totter, jerk.
And when I try to trace it back
To when I lost my dancing knack
It all points back, my dear, to you.
When you came out, out they flew!
It seems I lost them at your birth;
My tight slick moves of any worth,
And whilst I'm glad you're here with me,
I miss dancing wild, miss dancing free.

Birthday Un-lament

Don't lament your age today,
For give it a few years
When there's knees that crack at every move
And hairs sprouting from your ears
You'll cry out:
'I've lost my youth,
Oh no, I'm so perplexed!
How'd I get to this old age
That's left me rather vexed?

Take me back to that verdant time
When my youth was on display!
Well… compared to now at least!
Oh, I've frittered the years away!'

Please remember before you ruminate…
Today
You're as young
As you'll ever be.
So, celebrate your youth today,
even if you're ninety-three!

REASON 3:

SO MUCH STUFF IN THE WORLD

The Great Pacific Garbage Patch, floating in the Pacific Ocean, is three times the size of France. Fourteen million trees are cut down each year just to make paper bags. It's mind boggling just how much we are creating that eventually becomes waste.

We're encouraged to be more eco-friendly, but with green washing, how do we know if it's truly sustainable or not? A shirt made of '100% organic cotton' is supposedly sustainable because of the fabric, but can we really call an item of clothing that is made from a material which on average takes 20,000 litres of water to produce, 'sustainable'?

And it's not just greenwashing that causes me angst, but the actual amount of washing I have to do from all the clothes that I have previously bought unnecessarily!

Maybe the answer is not only to be more conscious about what we buy, but also to clear out what is cluttering up our lives. Is that so easy though? Do you get sentimental about your stuff?

Be a Litter Picker Upper

Be a litter picker upper,
Not a litter bug.
Forgo your take-out cuppa
If you've got no eco mug!

Swap your strawberries in December
For a dried apricot or two.
Go browse in local thrift stores
Before you rush for new.

Take your Tupperware to Tesco
For when you buy your cheese.
Go back to cotton hankies
To clear up any sneeze.

Reassess your portion size,
Don't just compost what's not eaten.
Grab an extra jumper
Before you up the heating!

Some days you may be hot on it,
Others a mild lukewarm.
We're not looking for perfection,
Just an improvement on the norm.

Each tiny change offers hope,
Don't you get the notion?
It's single drops of water
That make up any ocean.

Greenwashing

I'm so sorry to disabuse you of this misnomer in our lives,
But anything 'eco friendly' still has an impact that it hides.
Eco is, I'm sorry to say, not as eco does.
I know, that such a purchase may give an eco buzz,
But in all this eco buying there's a law that I must heed:
And that's to stop buying shit that I really just don't need.

The Séance

Oh bottom of the laundry bin,
Can you help us – are you there?
We've formed this séance to connect with you,
So, show yourself, please dare.

We remember when we saw you,
A familiar ally in our midst;
But we seem to have lost sight of you
With all these growing kids.

Have you passed to the other side?
Will we see you ever more?
We wash and rinse and spin the clothes
To try and see you like before.

The cards move around the table.
What is it that they spell?
'No, sorry love, 'til uni,
You're stuck in washing hell.'

All at Sea

The papers you poke at
Are not (in fact) a 'random pile',
But a telescope where I can look for miles;
Back to the things I may have missed,
When I mattered more, was less dismissed.

And that broken teapot
Is not (in fact) 'random tat',
But it takes me back to my first flat
With my only love when we laughed and laughed...
My teapot memory life raft.

And the fridge magnets and knick-knacks there
Are not (in fact) 'random clutter',
But memories that unfurl and flutter,
If I were to hold them in my hand;
Like lost treasure dug from within the sand.

The piles of books in every corner
Are not (in fact) a 'random selection',
But a faithful rudder aiding my direction.
Their words, coordinates to steer me on...
If I just had time to open one.

All this that you say must go
Is not (in fact) what's at stake,
But, like a boat creates a wake,
The consequence of my truth within;
That I'm afraid that I can't swim.

REASON 4:

HOW WE LOOK AT MENTAL HEALTH

As well as the Covid pandemic there is now talk of an anxiety pandemic. This brings me to number 4, which is the current way we look at mental health.

Anxiety, depression, addiction, many behaviours that are labelled as 'disorders' are manifestations of our nervous system being in fight, flight, freeze or flop because of what is going on around us. Yet with the medicalisation of our emotional states, we are convinced that we are disordered, rather than having a natural nervous system response to current or past threatening things in our lives.

Moving from a place of 'what is wrong with you?' to 'what has happened to you?' helps people to feel increasingly safe, if it is met without judgment or advice. If we keep on seeing the behaviour as the issue or labelling someone with a disorder, we may not see what is going on underneath.

The Expert

When we seek a diagnosis
Are we hoping for prognosis
In the handing to an 'expert' our 'true' fate?

I can't help but be suspicious,
Although the thought's delicious,
That a simple label helps improve my state.

The problem with this theory
Is it leaves me not to query
The God-like status that is given by default.

With their degrees and expertise
I should really feel at ease
That they'll combat my dis-ease
And make it halt.

And yet, the one that really knows me
That really holds the PhD
In the mystery of me...
Is me.

Labels

I am more than just a label that you try to pin on me!
My behaviour will betray me, if that is all you see.

You can try to reduce my being – call out addiction or OCD.
Dehumanise, pathologise, compartmentalising me.

I'm not a 'wash at 30' or 'fat content 3%'.
No. Labels are for objects, not breathing sentients.

I'm a human, whose emotional life's gone slightly out of whack.
Help me see my strengths and virtues so I can find my own way back...

...to the me I know that's in there when I peel away the pain.

I'm due my humanness – like you.
Underneath we're all the same.

Poppy

"Poppy's crazy! Poppy's cool!"

'Poppy sometimes bunks from school.'

(Poppy will back chat with passion.
Poppy has her own sense of fashion.)

"Poppy's crazy! Poppy's cool!"

'Poppy sometimes flunks at school.'

(Poppy lets herself in at night.
Poppy's parents scream and fight.)

"Poppy's crazy! Poppy's cool!"

'Poppy chooses to act up in school.'

(Poppy's dad looks at her that way.
Poppy knows what she mustn't say.)

"Poppy's crazy! Poppy's cool!"

'Poppy's to be expelled from school.'

(Poppy's secretly a secret keeper.
Poppy wishes she could've told a teacher.)

Poppy's crazy! Poppy's cool!

Poppy's safest place was school.

Max

'Max is quiet! Max is perfect!'

> (Max excels to feel he's worth it.
> Max has boarded since he was nine.
> Max is stoic; doesn't cry or whine.)

'Max has focus! Max has vision!'

> (Max is found doing his revision.
> Max knows to avoid the cupboard.
> Max acts like he isn't bothered.)

'Max is clever! Max is bright!'

> (Max swallows those screams at night.
> Max knows big boys don't cry.
> Max knows what he must deny.)

'Max is special! Max is wise!'

> (Max survives through perfecting lies.)

REASON 5:

NOT GIVING SPACE FOR PEOPLE TO

FEEL THEIR FEELINGS

If people take the brave leap into being curious about their feelings, in working on having more self-compassion and less judgment of themselves, they may find that the very thing they are fearful of, of feeling their feelings and being truthful about them, is what liberates them.

When I Say I'm Feeling Low Low

When I say I'm feeling low low
I need an
'Oh no! How so?
Let the tears flow! Have a good blow!'
That will let me know
That you know
That my low low
Will surely go,
'Cos I'm pro
At handling my low low.
I know it's just another
String from my long-ago-bow.
I don't need a 'should' show
Of 'out you go!'
Or a tell and show
Of how you overthrow
Your low low,
Or a 'just go with the flow'.
Let me so full
Of my woeful,
And in time, my
Low low will go.

Drowning to Live

As I stood at the shore of my memories,
As I prepared myself for the waves,
As the rollers crashed in with a thunderous roar,
So did the saltiness of those days.

I feared their size could drown me.
I feared I'd be swept out in the waves,
I feared for my life, for the heart of me,
I feared it was the end of my days.

For I'd given wide berth to the oceans,
I'd swum in the lakes, not the seas.
I'd swum in the pools and the rivers,
To tack my course with ease.

I feared the depths would drown me.
I feared I'd be swept out in the waves,
I feared for my life, for the heart of me,
I feared it was the end of my days.

But oh! The waves were distraction.
They knock you, but don't pull you down.
It's the current to watch, the riptide.
The currents that want you to drown.

But oh! To know that the drowning,
The strength of those currents deep down,
Is where you'll heal the yearning,
Is where salvation is found.

If You Need It Today

If you need it today: Yes always.
If you need it today: No never.
If you need it today: How could they?
If you need it today: How could you?
If you need it today: It's worth it!
If you need it today: It's not worth it!
If you need it today: Goof off!
If you need it today: Get serious!
If you need it today: You deserve that!
If you need it today: You don't deserve that!
If you need it today: This too shall pass.
If you need it today: It will never change.
If you need it today: Go!
If you need it today: Stop!
If you need it today: Me too.

REASON 6:

THE WORLD OF PUBLISHING

Twice (twice I tell you, *twice!*) I have made small mutterings to the publishing world that I have written things which I'd quite like to put into a book. This has not been well received.

The first time was when I had written five 'fake news fairy tales'. I took the traditional fairy tales and told them from the viewpoint of a character that you never hear of in the original tale. In these stories we heard from Mattress Mick, the mattress seller in *Princess and the Pea* and Amélie, the French cobbler who made the glass slipper for Cinders. I took them to a literary festival and spoke to some agents about them. They slated them.

However, it did lead to me writing and performing my first show. I thought, *When do you hear from those who are trying, but haven't made it yet; who aren't the J.K Rowling successes of this world, but are still giving it a bloody good go?* That was why I came up with the show 'Light in Life's Shadows', about the trickiness of being human.

The last time I spoke to an agent about my poetry they said to me, 'As soon as you said the word "poetry", I switched off.'

So, if you are reading this in a book it is because I decided to self-publish. That's how Margaret Atwood and Brené Brown started out, so I'm in good company.

Bitterness

I get it.
You're clever.
Well done.
Whilst I swing my way through
An obvious rhyme,
Your
Deep meaning
Brain steaming
Prize gleaming poems
Last and last and last
On published paper...
In bookstores...
Approved by agents and editors...
And *maybe* a reader or two...
I didn't want a book deal anyway.

To My Muse

Let me catch the words
Meant just for me,
Let me pluck them
From the air.
Help me weave them
With your guidance,
Help me sing
Your cosmic prayer.
Show the world
The deep truth
In the silence of the space,
Beneath the words you gift to me
With your presence and your grace.

A View on Poetry from My Teenage Self

Poetry makes me puke.
For starters, should it rhyme or not
To help you figure out the plot...
And meaning
That's hidden
Somewhere
Amongst the lines?
No, poetry makes me sick.
First off, I don't understand it
And isn't it all written by men who are
Dead
Or
In bed?
No, poetry is naff.
You won't catch me playing cat and mouse
With a motif
Or couplet
Or foot.
This poem is not clever,
'Cos poetry makes me puke.

Dragon Slayer

Don't let the
Nay Sayers
Be your
Dream Slayers,
Burning fledgling fantasies
With their
Dragon-breathed doubt.
Your idea
May have the
Body
Of a weak and feeble
'Just a thought'
But its
Heart and stomach
Has clout!

Keep Going

When you're full of self-doubt,
Keep going.
For there is no way of knowing
When your
Dream or aspiration
May take form.
Yet to be in the
Collective heartbeat
Of faith,
Holding yourself
With the tenderness
Of dawn light,
Will allow
Your purpose,
Your place,
Your unique imprint,
To show itself and
Leave the world in
No doubt.
You matter.

REASON 7:

APPARENTLY SOME OF US

DON'T MATTER

We live in a world which tells certain people that they don't matter because of the way they learn, or the colour of their skin, or the body they are housed in.

The first poem in this section I did actually write as I was matching socks. It's a particular bug bear of mine in a house where everyone's socks look very similar. As I matched the socks I thought about the futility of it, about how much of my time is wasted in order to get socks to match when, in actual fact, odd socks do just as good a job at keeping feet warm and protected.

It did make me think, though, about how much we unquestioningly veer towards some standardised 'norm'. In my original Odd Socks poem the word 'integration' was 'celebration'. I changed it after the Summer of 2020 when the resurgence of Black Lives Matter instigated a change in how I see the world.

You see, up until then I hadn't spent too much time challenging what the 'norm' was and who it benefited. As a cis, white, middle-class, heterosexual woman I was blind to the many privileges afforded me just by being born that way.

When we 'celebrate' people's differences, it still gives a nuance of a standard norm. What I'm learning is that celebration is important, but it doesn't go far enough. It still has a whiff of assumption, of 'Otherness'. It's why we have

Black History Month, rather than black pioneers, inventors, creators, leaders, kings and queens being taught about in our schools as a matter of course. We need to have both!

Of course, it's not just about race. Currently I think that we lack the vocabulary to be able to talk about these things in a humanistic way without being accused of being 'woke' because it has been so centred around where the power has been.

Until we can get under that, until we can stop othering and see the humanity in each and every one of us, regardless of our human tricky things, then integration is a challenge. We all love, hate, hurt, betray, because we're human, and it's recognising *that* that can unite us.

And I hear people say that they just aim to 'be kind', but if my view of what it means to be kind is influenced by my own view of what the norm is, how can I know that referring to something as exotic, or asking someone where they are from, or asking to touch someone's hair is not, in fact, kind at all?

Odd Socks

Who says that all our socks must match?
What if you'd grown up
With a batch
Of odd socks?
With such 'conformity', 'uniformity'
It's a self-fulfilling prophecy
Of them, not me…
Of other.
Oh bother!
I don't fit in,
I don't belong!
I must match by comparison!
If we'd been raised with integration
Of separate, unique differentiation
We'd accept the patterns and hues
Before we hid them in our shoes.
We'd appreciate the length, the colour,
If we'd been brought up not to bother…
About odd socks.

Tone Deaf

Oh I hear your symphony!
So I'll play along,
for I...
know this...
song.

A missed beat.
A dropped note;
White privilege learnt by rote.

Wrong pitch.
The timing's off.

A clattering crescendo.

A cacophony
of
just
white
noise.

For the way to train
my musician's ear
is to listen,
and not just hear.

Love And Light

Am I love and light?
Do I smite my spite?
'Accept' what's not right?
Keep it trite
In my aura of white?
Or do I go low
Into my shadow
To try to grow
From what I think I know?
So that I'm not just
A shit show with a rainbow?

Magazine Mantras

Younger and
Longer and
Beautiful and
Perfect and
Absolute and
Perfect and
Perfect and...
It's just one page
In a magazine.
Just one page.

True Self-love

I love my
Long legs
In the
Evening shadow.

The buoyancy
Of my boobs
In the bath.

The tight shape
Of my neck
When I lie down flat.

My
Just-watched-a-comedy
Laugh.

I love
My ears
Listening to my
Friend's sore woes.

My voice
Warbling a
Long-loved tune.

The hairs
From my 'tache
On a wax strip,

My skin by the light
Of the moon.

I may struggle to love me all the time,
May find something
each day to critique,

Or find a moment
where I choose to love
The fact that I'm unique.

Sunday Love Songs

Listening to Sunday love songs and the husbands writing in:
'She puts the whole family before herself, her priority's her kin!
These angels who walk among us, these selfless souls of love!'
I hear these words and I hear me say:

'Fuck that.'

I'm not chucking myself under a bus to get the world's admiration.
I've needs too, thank you very much, I'm not a martyr to the nation!

I'll happily hear anyone's needs – just alongside my very own.
I advocate equality in each and every home.

Fathers do not 'babysit' the kids whom they have sired.
Our default can't be 'You have it' so that we may be admired.

I'm loved for my consistency, my humour and my passion,
Not for any self-flagellation that gets labelled as 'compassion'.
Wake up to these toxic messages that subtly come our way,
To all of us alike – they've really had their day!

Insta-selfie-sation

Please tell me that I matter,
Please tell me that you care.
Please admire and envy me
As I pose in underwear.

Like me on my Insta
And share it where you can.
I'll take any likes on offer;
Even from that creepy fan.

You don't see my face
In my selfie that I post,
But come on, let's be honest,
That's not what matters most!

I'll do my squats to perk my butt
And tweak my cleavage right.
I'll strut and pose, no face exposed
And check my likes all night.

'Cos likes are what's important;
Followers I must accrue.
I'm an insta-selfie-sation
Fed by likes from you.

Free Thinking

My grandma called it word blindness, my mum 'dyslexia',
But I know that they got it wrong – I'm just a free-thinker!
Whilst neuro-norm go from A to B to get their answer quick,
I've gone to Z and J and P – but this is quite a trick...

We think outside the box you see,
I see things differently.
It's not much use in a spelling test,
But a gifted lot are we...

Think actors like Keira Knightly, Aniston and Bloom.
If only you'd see our talents – it's certainly not all doom.
Sportsmen like Lewis Hamilton and writers like good old Roald –
Seeing us as thickies in the class is really rather old.

Light bulbs were invented, Apple and Virgin too,
All thanks to our free-thinking; we're really quite a crew.
So don't see me for what I can't do, see me for what I can!
'Cos truth be told, we're rather bold, in the betterment of man.

Ok, so I say 'man' because it scans well, but I mean all humans of course!

The Dyslexic Kid

Don't mess with the dyslexic kid,
'Cos I know I have to work hard just to scrape by.
And I will!
For I am the tortoise when you are the hare.
So rest on your laurels and your neuro-norm thinking,
And one day, when you are least suspecting,
I may whip your butt
AND the score won't matter to me,
'Cos I took my pride in surviving the struggle;
In knowing that my worth is not
Wrapped up in the value of an exam score.

The Weed

I want to be a flower,
But it has been decreed
By some inhumane judgment
That I am just a weed.
I'm not in need of much to live,
Will flourish 'most anywhere.
I don't need special flower food,
I don't need special care.
Why is it that the fancy flowers
Are the ones that get attention,
Whilst me, tossed on the compost heap,
Don't even get a mention?

Lessons From Nature

The flower doesn't wilt and cry,
'I don't deserve the rain.'
The blackbird doesn't spend his day
In post worm-feast disdain.
The river doesn't shrink from the bed
That helps define its form.
The lightning doesn't doubt
If it belongs within the storm.
It's not nature's way to query any aspect of its worth.
So receive, give thanks and quit questioning whether you deserve.

REASON 8:

PEOPLE

While I'm all for people being treated equally, my number 8 reason why I want to stop the planet and get off is... people.

I think one of the benefits of lockdown for me was having that space and a slower pace of life. However, and I know I am contradicting myself here, without people we'd be bereft.

People help us feel like we belong, which we all need. It's people and community that get us though. Part of what was so difficult during Covid was not being able to be with people, especially when they were ill.

The Commute

I remember social graces
Before our phones were in our faces,
When we had a sense of
What was fine
And
What was not.

But now I'm on the train
And my god, it's quite insane,
As I sit right in the
Daily grind
Of
Social rot!

To watch that woman
Eating porridge…
To be honest
Is quite horrid,
As her open mouth
Churns and swirls
Her food.

Or the young mum doing FaceTime
(Well sure, she cannot waste time)
With her gynae, oversharing
Private news.

Whilst another plucks her chin!
What's this hellish world I'm in?
Is there nothing left
As a mystery in this life?!

That's all a bit mean really, because we've missed people, haven't we, when we've been in lockdown? And there's really nothing worse than feeling lonely.

I Am Lonely

Invitations to events (still waiting for mine)

Acting as if It doesn't really matter (but it does)
Meeting a 'how are you 'with 'fine '(but wishing they'd ask more)

Looking at myself in the mirror (asking: how did it come to this?)
Opening my mouth to say how I feel (but closing it again because I can't find the right words)
No one to tell 'I fed the dog '(or not even having a dog)
Edging on the periphery of conversations (I'm not a part of)
Looking at groups of other people (and asking myself, what do they have that I don't?)
Yearning to be someone's 'sight for sore eyes '(but we no longer even speak).

Belonging

The secret to belonging
Is to let your longing be.
Don't banish it far out of reach,
Exiled far from grace;
Beat the rhythm of its heart,
Trace the contour of its face.
For the secret to belonging,
Is to let your longing be.

REASON 9:

ILLNESS

I don't just mean Covid, but all the other illnesses that were still going on whilst Covid was happening. My friend was diagnosed with leukaemia in the autumn of 2020 and had to do her whole treatment in isolation, away from her family and friends.

In order to keep her going I wrote her poems. I wrote a letter to her leukaemia which is very rude, but these poems track the relentlessness of the chemotherapy and the misery of being ill. Sometimes there are no words to encapsulate the loss of a life that we were planning for, sometimes it needs space to fall apart, we need the space to be in the 'it's not fair'-ness of it all.

To Mr Luke Keemia

Read the room and take a hike.
In other words, be on your bike,
In other words, get out of here,
In other words, be on your ear,
In other words, you're not my sort,
In other words, get lost old sport,
In other words, time to go,
In other words, the answer's 'no'!
In other words, you're not my kind,
In other words are you fucking blind?
Read the room, you stupid cunt
You're to blame I got so blunt.

What Misery Is This?

What misery is this?
The fireworks are damp.
Butterflies have lost their lustre.
I've no joy that I can muster.
And now my mouth is chock to the brim of bloody painful ulcers.

What misery is this?
In the human race I'm losing.
Don't ask me to write a gratitude list,
It's a sure-fire way to encourage me to give you a proper bruising...

What misery is this?
Ooh I'm really getting going!
The world has gone to shit!
And on top of that...
I have no hair that's growing.

What misery this is!
Sympathy is a bitter pill.
It just reminds me I'm fucking ill.
Oh I know it's meant through your good will.
It's just, I'm crawling up this hill
With a rock sack on my back.

What misery is this?
Talking of rocks, I've hit the bottom.
My rock bottom is a shit storm flotsam,
Where no comfort's to be had.

What misery is this?
Oh when you ask I'll no doubt smile.
Tell you, 'I'll feel better in a while!'
Reassure *your* tears with, 'It's not that bad.'
The misery that's this.

Stop Telling Me

Stop telling me that 'you know'.
Stop telling me that 'you care'.
Just give me some peace as I work it out.
Please hide your puzzled stare!
I don't know the why or the how or the who,
But I'll work it out, I'll work it through.

Stop telling me it will pass.
Stop telling me I'm so strong.
Just give me some space as I stumble through,
As I pick apart what went wrong.
There may be some positive, that might be true,
But I'm not there yet, I've got to work it through.

It's Not Fair

Let me whimper into the pillow:
It's not fair.
Let me state it to the sky:
It's not fair.
Let me scream and shout,
Leave the world in no doubt
It's
Not
Fair!
It's not fair I'm woken for my vital signs.
It's not fair my pee's turned pink.
It's not fair that I'm force-fed pills and lines.
It's not fair I can't kick up a stink.
Let me declare out to the universe:
It's not fair!
Let me mirror my daughters' cry:
It's not fair!
Let me scream and shout, leave the world in no doubt:
It's
Not
Fair.
It's not fair I'm next to a chatterbox.
It's not fair that my temperature spikes.
It's not fair that I'm losing my golden locks.
It's not fair I can't go out when I like.
Let me get through this, each moment,
'Cos
It's not fair.
Let me hear those who cry with me:
'It's not fair!'
Let us scream and shout, leave the world in no doubt:
It's

Not
Fair.

And Then

There is a silence.

After the shock.

After it cracks, shatters, disintegrates
The life around you.
After the confused tumbling of your life that was.

There is a silence.

The free fall.

Where the truth whistles by:
Only in the falling do you fly.

REASON 10:

FEAR AND DESPAIR

Uncertainty often rides shotgun with fear and when that's ongoing it can rapidly inflate into despair.

It's excruciating to live with the not knowing, the not curing, the not healing. It's difficult when we are thrown into change that we did not choose. It's bewildering, shifting, like the world did a 180 flip with no warning.

Despair is lonesome.

Like I said at the beginning of this book, I have a choice about what to do when I feel fearful. In this section I address my fear and by doing that can recognise that there can be beauty to be found.

The truth is, we are all in this thing called life together and it's people, relationships and community that are our saving graces.

That's the reason that, after *all* the reasons that I have put into this book about leaving the planet, I'm staying around, because to stop the world and get off would be extraordinarily lonely and uninspiring. It'd be without people who are willing to stay with us in our darkest moments, those who bring joy into our lives and people in our local communities who continue to lead and inspire.

In the show I celebrated some of those people who are in my local community. Emma, who runs a bootcamp that I do; Clare, who started up a community fridge to reduce waste and help people who cannot afford food; and Lou, who has a group called Trauma Thrivers which encourages people to not only heal from their trauma but thrive through it.

The world has many confusing, horrifying, turbulent things going on right now, but the experience of being alive, being human, is made so worthwhile because of each other.

To My Fear

To the fear that says, 'Don't trust your life.':
Too late.
To the fear that cries, 'I keep you safe!':
How so?
To the fear that states, 'Without me is worse.':
Not true.
To the fear that claims my power and strength:
Fool's gold.
To the fear that shouts, 'Stay tiny and small!':
I rise.
To the fear that crows, 'You'll fail again!':
So what?

There Is Beauty In Despair

There is beauty in despair
For it speaks of a heart that loved so much,
Of an eye-watering longing
For a delicate dream that was dared.
Yes, look despair square on and say
It's only because I cared!

Resolve

I start from where I am today
And tomorrow,
Well, that's another day,
For I can only work with what I've got
And let time tell
If that's enough to not,
But it's all I have,
So I'll go from here.
I'll lean more to faith
And less to fear.
Even when it's
With a heavy heart,
Let me find a way
To make a start.

Our Moonlit Path

I said, 'Oh it'd be lovely,'
And you said, 'Sure it'd be grand,'
And we went off into the sunset
Walking hand in hand.
But as the sun set, it brought shadows;
Made monsters where once it seemed safe.
They looked like our childhood nightmares,
In which we were always chased.
I said, 'Oh it's so scary,'
And you said, 'Look at the stars,'
For we're in this together, for always,
Walking our moonlit path.

Don't Jump In The Puddles!

Don't jump in the puddles!
Why skip in the rain?
Don't stare in the distance!
Must I tell you again?

Must you shove in your food
With such vulgar haste?
It goes down so quickly!
How can you taste?

Don't leave your coat when you go outside!
When I call you to come, why must you hide?
Must you poke that snail into its shell?
No, it's not funny when you make that smell!

Why must you be so troublesome, boy?
'Cos Mum,'
he chuckles,
'I choose Joy.'

The Surrey Community Fridge

As the earth is going solar
There's a situation that is polar
Right here behind closed doors in Dorking town.
As Bob and June and Jo last week
Simply didn't have a bite to eat.
Unable to buy food (it'd get you down),
Whilst a surplus of green smoothies
And Easter eggs with themes of movies
Are on the verge of being chucked away for good.
A team of two are on a mission
To rotate food back to the kitchen,
That's otherwise wasted in our hood.
Ten tons of food per week
Is delivered to those who seek
A respite from hunger through the situation that they've been dealt.
Community fridge is a saviour,
To our own and to our neighbours.
It's enough to make your own heart melt!
So give a cheer or more support
For what started as a thought
Is now a hundred-strong team of volunteers.
Fourteen hours every day,
Claire and Tony's mission is underway.
Thank God for these inspiring pioneers!

Middle-Aged Bootcamp

We became Emma's squaddies
To get some fitter bodies,
To handle our frenetic busy lives.
Some have injured shoulders,
Others don boulder holders,
But we ignore these facts
As we breathlessly high five.
Claire nails the plank press-up,
Kate adjusts her moon cup,
While a few run off to pee behind the hedge.
Emma's mantra is quite direct,
But it has the right effect:
'Do you wanna get fit,
for that is what I pledge.'
It's a good point entirely,
I block out my future diary
To prioritise these fun sessions with this squad.
It's not just fitness that I've gained,
But uncliquey mates, come shine or rain.
So let this poem give you a loving gentle prod.
Come outside and join in!
Ditch the cold harsh-lighted gym,
Having fun with fitness is always such a plus.
So come on now, please sign up,
Come and join this merry line-up.
There's a place for you,
You'll fit right in with us!

Trauma Thrivers

When I'm feeling befuddled or muddled or blue,
Missing the love and respect I deserve.
I remind myself of what's right and what's true
And delve into my inner reserve.

I know I'm fucking fantastic you see.
And reasons? I've got them galore!
I did more than survive; a thriver, that's me!
A thriver I truly adore.

I cartwheel, refurbish, break cycles of pain,
I crack jokes in languages new.
I rap and set boundaries and daily abstain.
Paint murals, find answers anew.

For arseholes, I find some compassion,
Run marathons, and can always find home.
I wild swim and windsurf with passion,
And leave narcissists all well alone.

I'm present when my kids bring their issues,
I'm loyal, brave and a badass to boot!
And even when I'm tired to my tissues,
Thriving's my eternal pursuit.

I know I'm fucking fantastic you see.
And reasons? I've got them galore!
I did more than survive; a thriver, that's me!
A thriver I truly adore!

As I draw near to the finish of this, I hope that you are left feeling like you are part of something much bigger than just you, wherever you are. You are part of the human community and your actions, large or small, have an impact on others that you can't even imagine.

I hope my poems help you to realise and remember that.

Finally, I hope that this book brings you some sense of hope, and can help you find your own reasons for staying around. Because it would be incredibly lonely and uninspiring without you.

The Gift of Poetry

Please receive my words as gifts,
Each poem a billet doux.

Each line a delicate heartstring
To see the tough times through.

Please feel the feelings from these words
As small squeezes of your hand;

A gesture of solidarity –
Not too fancy, nor too grand.

That all I'm ever trying to say,
All I want to do

Is encourage you to be who you are…
To be the youest you.

The Hunt for Hope

I hunted for hope in the cupboard.
I looked for it under the stairs.
I searched for hope in the cookie jar.
I sought it in strangers' stares.
I asked about hope at lost property.
I checked my inbox in case.
I poked about under the sofa.
I even went through the waste.
But it was masterly sequestered.
Its camouflage had me tricked.
I was on the edge of despairing,
When something inside me clicked.
I glimpsed it in the squirrel,
Who simply cared not a jot
About whether 'my life' as I'd wanted
Would go ahead or not.
I caught a peek through the spider's web,
Such beauty from something I'd shun.
I glanced at the hint of suggestion
That came from the winter's sun.
I peeped at it in the planets,
That made me feel so small
And this lit something inside of me,
For none of it matters at all.
For we are alive and that's magic!
A once in a lifetime chance!
And I caught hope by the hand again
And I asked it once more to dance.

ACKNOWLEDGEMENTS

It's hard to track back exactly how something comes about, but there are definitely people who have inspired me or been my cheerleaders along the way in the writing of this book.

When I was a child my mum bought me a book called 'I like this poem'. It introduced me to poetry and that first introduction helped me see that poetry could be fun and accessible and that you could like a poem before you could understand it.

Barbara Sorensen, for appreciatively listening to many of my poems before they were out in the world, which gave me the confidence to share them with a wider audience. Lisa & Thomas Soede, Alex Saunders, Susan McGrath, David Scoffield, Lorraine Isles, Omikemi Natacha Bryan, Megan Febuary, Miles Adcox and Dr. Brad Reedy who have all encouraged and supported me. Those who have attended my therapeutic writing workshops (and given me such lovely testimonials). Susan Earlam for taking the time to walk me through the world of self-publishing. Terrell Lewis for lending me some self-belief whilst I went about creating my own and for your own poetry and your grace. Suzanne Hume, for inspiring so many poems about cancer and for helping me figure out how I was going to come onto the stage for my show 'Stop the World, I Want to Get Off'.

Thanks to the writing group headed up by the inimitable Melanie Whipman and all the talented writers whom I have met there – especially Kari Gillespie and Emma Wood (thank you for reading this before it went to print and giving me such wonderfully helpful feedback).

The fabulous people of Dorking: Isabel Morris, who created 'Dorking is Talking', a spoken word supper club (as lovely as it sounds), thank you for giving me my first paid gig and for creating such a supportive atmosphere for fledgling writers and seasoned performers. Mary Huggins and Claudia Cartwright at Mole Valley Arts Alive. Emma Harrison and her squaddies, Clare Davies and Lou Lebentz who inspired some of the poems in this book.

Finally, but by no means least, I want to acknowledge my delightful sons Alex, Jake and Harvey – for coming along to my first reading and staying there, even though I mentioned the word 'boobs'. I think you are amazing, each in your own unique way and it is my absolute privilege to be your mum. And to my husband David for coming to listen to my poetry, even though poetry makes you puke!

ABOUT THE AUTHOR

Jacky Power MSc is an addiction psychologist, poet and host of The Therapeutic Poet Podcast. She lives in the Surrey Hills with her husband, three boys and chocolate Labrador. She's on a mission to use her poetry to help people understand and express their feelings, or, as she says, 'rehumanise us one poem at a time'.

www.ingramcontent.com/pod-product-compliance
Lightning Source LLC
Chambersburg PA
CBHW041148110526
44590CB00027B/4161